CROSSROAD MIRROR

CROSSROAD MIRROR

POEMS

HUSSAIN AHMED

Curbstone Books / Northwestern University Press
Evanston, Illinois

Curbstone Books
Northwestern University Press
www.nupress.northwestern.edu

Copyright © 2026 by Northwestern University. Published 2026 by Curbstone Books / Northwestern University Press. All rights reserved.

Printed in the United States of America

10 9 8 7 6 5 4 3 2 1

Library of Congress Cataloging-in-Publication Data

Names: Ahmed, Hussain, author.
Title: Crossroad mirror : poems / Hussain Ahmed.
Description: Evanston : Curbstone Books/Northwestern University Press, 2025.
Identifiers: LCCN 2025016600 | ISBN 9780810149304 (paperback) |
ISBN 9780810149311 (ebook)
Subjects: LCGFT: Poetry.
Classification: LCC PR9387.9.A362 C76 2025 | DDC 821.92—dc23/
eng/20250409
LC record available at https://lccn.loc.gov/2025016600

For Officer S.
and the Nigerian Army

I was born in a North that burns;
I have not lived in one that doesn't.

CONTENTS

INCANTATION FOR A LAKE

In this picture, I walked   down the steps
into a lake,   dressed   for a funeral
except no one I knew died   but the numbers   rose
from the right corner of the TV screen.

Before I left my room,   Baba called
asking   if they would let me cross the border back home

                if they have found a field to bury all the dead,

                if they now let people warm their lovers' palms one last time

or   if they let them have their ashes.

South of this lake,
a shepherd dog   guards a car cemetery.
        I understand
its tired eyes know   coyotes don't eat metal scraps.

        The dog would be happier
in a farm   than here,
        where every bent rim
or cracked rearview   is proof of scars and memories.

My wrists were tied
behind my back

with a tesbihi
or guitar strings.

Anytime I tried
        to wriggle it off, it vibrated
and the dog came running toward me.

In a small office
packed with faulty speedometers, a man made a gun joke—
I showed him my palms.

I surrendered my brown rosary to his mouth
and he chewed on it, as I counted my regrets
for coming this far away
from the lake, away
from the room where I kept count
of the dead numbers as they climbed.

I collected my regrets
like dew on the grasses in my backyard,
where no one mowed for months.
We were unsure where the virus bred.

CHIMERA (PALM AND WINE)

This house is an incubator   for spiders.
Memories are gardened inside the cracked walls.

I heard this story from a blind palmist who spoke
through his son,   unconscious—after gulping brews

of fermented millets.   Surrounded by landmines
in a field that bordered ghost villages in Gwoza.

I beseeched the palmist to tell of what lies ahead
of these towns and their lonely pigeons.

There is an end to this war, but   its fracture could
be permanent   and there is danger in permanence.

I grabbed a handful of the wind,   my fingers floated
in what should have been resistance.

Since a dead fish houses a liverwort seedling,
not everything that floats is dead.

Every plant that grows on a brown river
surely has its roots in the mouth of a ghost.

Until then, the gurney was returned
to the safe house behind the mosque.

Now, I stomach my nostalgia for the towns I won't
get to love.

In the corner of a room lies a prayer rug,   shrunk with fire.
The prayers of the old tenants lingered   somewhere above
the roof.

The prayer mat they left behind is a diary of how long
they've had their foreheads hennaed in praise of the unseen.

Today, I pray for this city to be safer than its seas,
so there would always be a place to hide

and every lost body would be found. For now, incense
glows from my tongue, before it runs out of wishes.

INCANTATION FOR THE DROWNED

The sea knew my ancestors
from their yearly   pilgrimage,

but it was the birds
that called me   by their lost names.

Everything I know about drowning,
I learned

from men who survived
the flood   as boys.

In the backyard, a mango   gets closer to rot
when it ripens.   I blame

the sun, because God created
everything sweet   with guilt,

and every cracked wall sings
of the drowned   nomads.

When I had the courage
to leave   home,

I memorized the names of the missing.

CHIMERA (LIGHT AND PRAYERS)

We rely on the sky   for prayer time.

A parrot on the balcony   won't stop

singing in its cage.   It curses

and prays   for every stranger.

I know I am a stranger   in this country.

I don't feel guilty   when I miss jummah prayers.

I fear the adhan would slip   beneath the heavy doors,

and a stranger would knock   on the front gate,

asking why there's a God whose tongue they cannot mimic.

GRAY

I know what a body emptied
of its light feels like on the palms.

I have seen a body emptied of
its memory. I dread the open eyes,

even though I don't dream of them—
I dread what is dead that is not a sacrifice.

I avoid eyes emptied of light. I fear
they would tell me something new about myself

if our eyes meet. I am scared they will
tell me what no one would believe.

I am not bold enough to be a mad prophet.
Today, I locked eyes with a small body

emptied of want. The toddler was younger
than the one I held to the cemetery in these hands

because we don't have gurneys for children.

I dream of bodies cloaked for prayers,
laid on the gray rug inside my room.

I'm waiting for my brothers to join me
as we always do, but they are seven seas away

and this prayer must be said before the sunset.

The moon is God's right eye.
We don't bury our dead under its light, even in war.

I was alone, but I heard my lover's voice
asking me to switch off the fan.

With eyes eclipsed with fatigue, I raised my hands
and brought the blades to a halt

after watching the clips of children
dressed as if they were on a journey in the Sahara,

except their mothers are assembled
in a garden of wrens, learning to perfume their palms

with what is left of their dead.

CHIMERA (SCENT AND MEMORY)

There's a cap in Baba's wardrobe.
It doesn't fit his head   but
it was uniformed

    for a wedding he missed.
    His memories are dated
    in two calendars.

No one
would inherit this cap.
It's also a bag

    for passport photographs
    or old currencies
    or expired drugs.

It stores
all the al-miski perfumes
to soften the stillness of the dead.

    Every Friday,
    he scents himself
    as we do with the dead bodies.

This ritual
reminds them
of all they left behind

    to remind them
    of what they've practiced on how
    to answer Munkar and Nakir.

We gather
to warm their cold bones
with praises

of the generations
that are no more—
and pray

that the scent of al-miski
guides them home.

ASHES

Scars made a family of men who were once
strangers.
In many years, their paths would not
cross, except on a deserted alley
where they would stare into the halogen
lamps and march on.

There is a demise of a soldier that you may read on
your way to the kitchen
or on the radio after a music break. It will
break you
for now, you are a branch of dead
figments, smothering in a tunnel.

Henceforth, all the dead would live in you.

And you would live in someone who saw your face in a
photo album
or heard of how you rescued a family of rabbits on
the battleground.

You would live in the body of a stranger, who watched how
you fed the rabbit
and her seven kits slices of mangoes you
ripened in powdered charcoal.

DEPARTURE

Sometimes,   you would lose a friend   in an ambush.

You would fight off the fog   that clouded the bank
  of your eyes.

It's not only the dead   and their laughter   you had grown
  used to,
it is the wives   that would call your number
  to confirm if it was true,
and their children   who knew you from the picture
  you snapped
        on the last Eid.
Their families are now yours   and you are   a galaxy
for wandering satellites   torching the edges of the dark field
  with matchsticks.

In the picture,   you pinned a ram to the ground
  and smiled.

You may have removed the ram's horns   after singeing,
  to breathe in the hot air.
        Baba said it cures epistaxis.
No one we knew was healed,   but we believed
      in the miracle of a ram's horn.

Sometimes, you lose a comrade in a gunfight,   but you continue to
  finger the trigger,
    like a prayer bead.
You won't lower your gun;   you must live to mourn the departed.

CIRCLE

There's no vocabulary   in the army—   for grief,
    or death.
Each door you exit,   leads
    to another parade ground.

With each lightning   on the face of the sky,   you
    remember
the matching tattoos   you drew   on each other's
    backs.

The flash   of repeating memories you crave
    every morning,
I hope it keeps you alive   until the next
    gunfight.

Every death is expected,   but you loam the pains   in your
    mouth
and sing   of the days when the gyration was
    enough
for you   and the battalion.   You remember
    ________________,
excused from the war front,   and like you,   he
    envisaged rapture.

The roaring of the waters   on the edge of Lagos
    reminds him of Maiduguri,
the thatch   where you both kept watch   and sang until it
    stopped raining.
The ocean's wave   kept him alive
    until the next gunfight.

He returned before the arc on his stomach
healed.

The field is where the love is; he made it to the
pavilion
where you both sang at the top of your voices, because
you must not close your eyes,
not in prayers, not to dream of anywhere outside
the circle.

After the ambush you
still hear whispers
of his songs; that alone keeps you too alive until
the next gunfight.

UNMARKED

They pointed your wife to a mound of clay marked with
Coca-Cola bottle,
your name written hurriedly on a piece of paper
inside of it.

Baba escorted her to the burial ground
with your daughter.
Until she came for you, you were declared
missing.

Everyone is declared missing until declared dead.
No one would tell her
how you died, and she would not ask— she saw
the pictures—
you were laid beside another soldier in full
regalia.

A giant mango tree stood tall by the entrance. It casts
a shade on the
signboard with the invocation to be muttered before they
entered the burial ground.

The shadow was a trap for the promise that followed, In sha
Allah—bikum laa'ikun.

She doesn't understand the language she prayed in;
your daughter does,
but she's tired of the moving car. She wanted to return
to the barrack,

to stare at your pictures when there's no one close by.
She wants to be unmarked
in the room she was born in, the room where we last sat
around a tray of jollof rice.

NORTH

We passed the Fields of Gazing Grain—
We passed the Setting Sun—

—Emily Dickinson

Inside an ark, heading to a shore   littered with strangled
    sharks,
        a cactus unfroze   and began to bloom.

That day, tents in a desert were mistaken   for insurgent
    hideouts,
        a bomb dropped   inside the hospital—

just before a woman sang her child   to sleep.
        In a white jellabiya,   he was dressed for prayer.

The rain softened the ground   because every transition has an end.
        She recited   ayatul kursiyi.

Her opened palms were slates   for names she saved for her unborn
    children
        before a gallon of gasoline was mistaken for Zamzam.

BIRTHMARK

Another girl on a gurney / her stomach
now an empty threat / like a pear without its pit.

She lost her life / for another / to come alive.

Here / a man does not cry when a woman dies / in a labor room;
he marries another before the start of harmattan.

Every man tells me not to fear the syringe.
They tell fables of how strong they were at my age.

No one ever catches me when I cry after another girl's Janazah.
I do not expect any pain to ring through my joints
while leafing through the pages of my mother's diary.

My mother's breasts swell when other children cry,
but when I took my first step / a week after I stopped crawling, /
there was a man at the gate / asking to take me to custody.

There is a dying lantern inside our room, / it blurs
the faces of all the women who surround me.

I remembered a friend who died with an infant's feet between her legs.
I never asked whether she was buried with her legs closed. /

Here / our women survived cold wars
because of the enamel plates in their breast pockets
that kept them safe from the straying bullets. /

The girls inside the theater are mathematicians.
They modeled formulas to calculate the inches
of their husbands' penises. /

A child's cry brought songs to their lips;
they recited verses of the Qur'an that sound like poetry.

One of them held the child's leg and touched his head to the ground. /
Three weeks away / it will be another girl in her mother's skirt.

It will be your turn to tell her to push / to keep breathing.
Before then / another girl will be buried / and another married off.

TAXONOMY: GRIEF

It is noon and there's grief in the air.
A girl surrounded by elephants three times her age,
their tusks bent toward the sky as if in supplication.

There's a seat for everyone because it's no taboo
for women to mourn.   She walks down the aisle alone
despite her shoulder blade   heavier with each step.

The mourners are hungry,   but it's a taboo
to ask for food   when the deceased had no gray hairs.

The echoes in your stomach tell of how empty
you have become. You emptied your bladder through your eyes;
your body is now 30 percent water   and 70 percent salt.

On the bench   she remembers how they met,
the curl of his lips when he called her name.

The forecast on the radio claimed it would rain—   it did not.
This could be another bad dream she doesn't want to see.

For too long   she wants to give the women her eyes.
She feels a pulse farther from her rib cage   just below her navel,
where she hopes to get a tattoo of his name   scribbled in red.

AUTOBIOGRAPHY INSIDE A CHURCH

For Ozubulu

Where I'm from, there is no winter;
it's either flooding or burning.
A bell rings inside an empty cathedral.
Soon, feathers grew on my arms
until the bullets pierced the silence.
I knew nothing about writing eulogies for the dead
as men who are gatekeepers in a military cemetery.
There are perfect days to die and perfect seasons for burial,
but this country only mourns those who died on weekends.
My parents taught me the art of prayers.
I don't have to lose a finger before I confess a sin—
and I never get trapped within the chaos of tongues.
My parents taught me to say *surrender* in a foreign language.
When I close my eyes to pray, I do not see angels bidding my gun.
I see my parents reading from another volume of—
[how to safely throw stones in a glass house].
The bell rings the second time.
I hope my confessions made it beyond the chandelier
before they got stained in blood.
Beads on tiles, the cathedral continued its silence.
As we count the dead, the pew smells of blooming tulips.

BIRDS

Today an egg hatched,
and the sky awaits its induction.

The sky kept record of all that flew on it,
but doesn't tell when they go missing.

Emerged from the ashes were feathers
with faded inscriptions of Baba's will, on interlocked barbules.

Owls' alternating calls were mistaken for the muezzins.
They lodged in the minaret while we were on curfew.

There is a scar on my back; I can't recall how I got it,
or any other healed wound on my body.

Here, birds do not earn their names by how high they fly.

RADIO

Baba's house was a box-shaped percussion
stringed with stories of war and music.

Spoils of war were made into gowns for survivors.

Ẹni tí yio royín ógún koni b' ogún lọ́. On the wall, there
was a clock with the face of Queen Elizabeth.
I once thought she sang the iqama when it was time for
prayers.

Fascinated by this miracle, we played war games.
We connected tins with thread and sang through them.

There were pictures in empty wine bottles floating on a
river.
The moon was a witness to the end of this love story.

When we left home, I made space
in my bag for the wall clock.

Ghosts continue to lurk in Baba's box of grief and blues.
The clicking hands of the clock helped track his
breathing.

TELEPATHY

His face darkened
by the entrance of a lighthouse.

Baba's eyes danced
to songs he'll never sing aloud.

On his forehead is a harmony
for fast notes—or a map

to an ark built for all he owned
that survived the fire.

In his eye sockets were a gallery
for baroque paintings,

concealed in Zukhruf
but stained in blood.

He sat on a wooden box
the size of a toddler's coffin.

In it, he saved birth certificates
and vaccination receipts.

Because ao gbòdò fi
ohun afẹ̀ k' ọmọ jogùn ra iná,

he glued an amulet on the padlock.
It is sacrilege to open it in his absence.

He says he loves me; I imagine
it is untrue—because I can't fit in his box,

and he sings of darkness, as I would
of a peach ripened by sun.

Though his body is neither stranger
to silence nor grief,

his philtrum is the tip of a spear
before it touches blood.

I want to tour the ark before it sails,
so I'll know all he's trying to save

from this withering sky,
from the approaching storms.

MOONQUAKES

1.
Eagles were scattered on the ashy sky,
paddling the air with barbed toes on the eve of an eclipse.

2.
The moon is like fermented honey in a glass ball,
new shadows emerged when it quaked.

I watched as the stars fluctuated in countless congregations.
I prayed against this omen of an eclipse on a Friday.

3.
I made it to the beach for the first time after I lost my friend.
A priestess raised a cup of gin to her lips as the tides approached.

For years, I did not set foot inside any river.
I fear the grief I hold in my bones may sprout.

REFLECTION

There is a feather in us all,
but mine often
reroutes me back home.

The day after a flood, our room sounds emptier
than it was before we slept.
I wondered what we lost to the brown water.

Like the glittering lips of a knife that turns rusty
in a pouch that is to keep it safe,
our shadows became translucent on the blue wall.

This is how I imagine the bottom of the sea,
but layered with stones
or crab bones—

where an octopus hides, waiting
for prey to wander into its territory.

WAVES

As new song brews
from the tides of the ocean,
the vibrations put octopuses to sleep.

You may see the shadow
of Saro-Wiwa waiting
to teach you how
to purge salts lodged in bones.

The ocean
encroached the neighborhood
in the night.

You must learn to swim,
until each of your rib bones softens—
in memory of men the ocean swallowed,
men who yelled for rescue.

The ocean lost its salt
and its hue.
It would take more than a field of mustard
to reverse the oil spillage.

As the leaves fluttered in the wind,
the ghosts of the dead sang the ocean to stillness.

BEACH

Away from the water,
I led soldiers in prayer.

There were no tags on their chests,
and no ranks. I have seen them before,

or maybe they were healers
in God's many faces.

Unmarked graves
in the military cemetery—

a gully in a garden of sunflowers.
We shook hands after the prayers.

Two weeks ago,
I woke up to the demise

of a friend that was down on typhoid.
He was there too,

in a caftan I never saw him wear
before I left home.

I called his name for one last time.
He answered—surprised.

There's a catalog
for dead things in my mouth.

On a hallowed grassland,
I kept running until my legs disappeared.

The beach may have been encroached then, but now
we stand in perfect rows before sunrise.

Naked on a hot bank of a salted water,
history will recall this moment as moderate and deadly.

It is the first of such—
proximity of grief and beauty.

The skin continues to glimmer,
smeared with shea butter.

Wet air will blow off the sea,
and the tides will continue to fall anytime they hit the rock.

LANTERN

We own a sacred lantern,
but I don't know its origin.

Its glass made room for our images
without burning them.

Once, it lost its praise to the sun
because it was lit

in the afternoon, after
a new child was born.

I grew up to be the lamp bearer.
I washed the glass

until it was bright as a toddler's eyes
opening for the first time.

This was my earliest memory of love.

I want it to hold my reflection longer
as it eats up the darkness in the mosque

where our names were announced
to a sleepy congregation after subhi.

When the light slithered through
the window, my brothers' voices heightened.

Because now, Baba would know who
said the zikir with their eyes closed.

I held the lantern firmly in my hands
and watched as darkness unfurled

from an unfinished prayer house.
I joined the circle, as we'd done

until the war, before the sky became
a pollen-basket swamped with stingers.

YORUBA ABECEDARIAN

Assembled in a field of
browning cornstalks,

dozens of soldiers huddled around a faulty compass,
entranced by their urge to dance to bullet songs.

Ẹgùn kî mu ọjọ́ so l'okùn, not even
for the amulets around their wrists, they

gawked at the sky for floating feathers, because
gbangba l' aṣá tá fún ọmọ akín.

Hunted, the birds forgo their songs, but
in their silence is a ritual for the missing. They

joined the sides of their palms together, but
knew when to keep their eyes open in prayers.

Lost in the Gwoza forest, they left me a message.
Months after it was sent, I became an eagle

nutmegged in currents of strong winds, but
ornamented with the scriptures of lost shepherds.

Ọgbẹ ọkàn le mú ni fuyé jú òwú tú tú ló
pressed into a tent, to hide the soldiers from rain.

Regiments of sacred men, waiting for the war to end,
sonorously, they sing the praises of their lovers.

Ṣugbọn omi àdágún ko le ya àwòrán aláṣọ̀ ala.
Thrown inside a cave with a fork to dig up an exit

under the tent, water runs against their feet.

What a mirror does not show
yearns to remain wrapped in shadow.

*This abecedarian is written in the Yoruba alphabet.

MONOLOGUE IN A LIBRARY

Piles upon piles, books in foreign languages,
their titles concealed by dust.
This man did not remember   what stories lay
in the brown pages of his own library.
The radio is without the antenna, the cloggy screen
of the television—capable of only silhouettes.
Where I come from, silence is how you mourn a man without
gray hairs. When you speak, you tell his children
their father had joined the army; you tell lies in his wake.
Baba failed many times to recall who I was
or why I had refused to laugh at his jokes,
as veins stretched along the walls of his temples.
He bought the first book a week before he got married.
Baba dreams in different languages we don't understand.
Another of his sons died, two years after his wife.
No one wants him to know what happened, but
he is regaining his memories from the images on the wall.

PALSY

For A.

This room is the ring where he fights all the matches
without gloves. If it rains when the stars are out,
the night sky will be the wrong place to search for light.
His fingers are slender inflorescences
or quenched stars but not withered crinum.
The therapist   prescribed water when his temperature rises.
It was in the hospital that he noticed   his shadows have
  outgrown him.
His cracked knuckles became spinnerets, and
the woven nest cannot hold eggs until they hatch.
Every day for a year, he trains for a next match
until the sun comes out again tomorrow. His eyes are
gray around the irises   like chalcedony
held toward the center by chalaza or maybe silk.
He had only one victory   celebrated for too long.
He recognizes a satellite from the many stars that litter the sky.
He was cheered for another triumph.
He could differentiate between colors that his father was blind to see.
Between bubbles, he called out our names.
He asked if I would teach him poetry, so I bought him a ballpoint.
We wrote epiphanies to our mother.
I wonder if she's happy to have died before all her children.
I feel empty reading the words in search of errors.
I feel betrayal, like having shoes no one ever sees you wear.
This boy has become a shadow   squeezed beneath the black of
  our curtain.
He wants a face for the voice that woke him   when it
  rained.
The blanket does not warm a motherless child, and hot tea cannot do
  the magic.
Our mother's perfume lingers in her room, and I sometimes think
she is not gone, maybe, she would be back anytime soon.
My brother   faces the Kaaba,

with his legs coiled beneath him. He raises his hands
to his ears and back to his thighs. He is cold, he was born cold.
He asks if men can grow wings and not be angels.
He closes his eyes when he prays,
I imagine that's the only time he sees himself standing with no aid.
When he opened his closed eyes, I saw an eagle perched
inside the moon, ready to soar higher.
I light up incense when he pronounces another word correctly.
The flood left us empty, but the ground is dimpled.
My brother and I filled the potholes with the broken plates.
I must admit, we lost our mother the second time five years after
the first.
We changed the paint in her room   from yellow to blue.
Her ghost slithers through the curtains,
to the space between a satellite and a star, somewhere in the night sky.

FENCE: AN ABECEDARIAN

A mile from where I once spent a night,
bees lodged beneath a bald cypress—in a
city I know but not too well to
dream about its blue sky with eyes closed.
Every cloud is shaped like a mausoleum
forged from cotton candy—or Galanthus
grown in a park, deserted even on
holidays. It's hilly from here on.
I climb slowly and read the names
jostling to remain legible on the signs. I
know this would remind me of something
lost, something I no longer wish to own.
Many nights, I imagined I heard
noises from the other side of the fence.
Out through the window, I whistled,
paced the kitchen, and waited for a response—but
quit when I remembered that was how we summoned snakes. The room
reeked of scents from hundreds of gladioli,
seeded by mourners who may never return
to water the field. On the other side is a bouquet of memories
unraveling in the summer's heat. For now, I am a
victim of my own empathy. I
wrote my dream on the bathroom wall,
xylographed with strangers' names. For
years, I dreamt of that room. If the wall stays unpainted a
zillion years away, I'll be alive in the eyes of strangers.

COMPASS

Squirrels rustled the dried leaves
that carpeted the backyard. The sun
remained whole throughout
the season. I craved the pool
ornamented in blue lights.

At the entrance of where I lived,
I sat beside the water
every night after I lost the salt
in my body, lifting dumbbells
to country music—my country's music.

Pointing at the night sky, a stranger asked
if I knew what planets aligned
with the moon. I told him I only know the moon
because it is a compass for the holy month
of Ramadan.

In harmattan, no one would sit by the ocean.
Its salt reminds them of the pilgrims who never
returned—reminds them of their faded laughter.

ZUIHITSU

I know what becomes of the tongue after
prayers: It craves a bird.
A man I had not seen for years brought guinea fowls, their
legs tied.

I have no story of their crests, but their eyes wandered as I
once was—
unsure if the dark sky is of dawn or surging rain.

Once, I trusted my image to a mirror that is uncapable of reflections.
I trusted a blade I used to sharpen my raffia pens
and cut my nails.

It is a ritual tto feed what we must sacrifice. Each time,
I watch from afar— I would have been closer if it
was a ram.

It is no fun to watch light slip out of feathers
but there is no restriction to my urge for a miracle.

The second bird was numb on the cracked cement floor.
The water in a bowl to appease its spirit was
untouched.

In few flaps, it landed on the kitchen's roof— in our open
compound.
It stood on the corrugated sheets, flexing its feathers

as it decided whether to go in the direction of the
wind.

It was my exam week;   it was Baba's dream that I join the
    Nigerian Army.
    I was unbothered;   I would rather die with a raffia pen in my
        hands   than a gun.

This I could not tell Baba,   for he stayed up in the night
    and called on our ancestors   to intercede
        on my behalf.

I heard him whisper into the night's wind for days.
My hand wielded a pen and upheld the names of our dead.

INCANTATION FOR LEAVING

It gets better from here, say
the dead, who must remain silent

in solitary re-living of memories,
until the trumpet is scrubbed

of its rust, and maybe painted
to hide its deficiency.

Leaving never gets better.

A boy who survives drowning says
the sea is saltier than it looks.

I won't get to know that,
I'll blame the coldness,

and the guilt of what is
hidden in its blue.

Leaving never ends—for now,
I rest my tired wings

and lubricate my tongue
with the filtrates of soiled prayers.

GRAVITY

To know what happens
        when you meet the aliens,

to know you once named me
        that which you now seek,

knowing that I am not from Mars.

To know that God is a weapon
        in your vocabulary,

to know you would introduce them
        to what you have never seen,

to know you expect them to
understand your accent.

In space, black is a shape
and coincidentally,

it also means disappearance.

It is how you know someone is lost
and would never return.

To know what happens
when you meet the first aliens,

to be sure, seduce them with apple juice,
or force it down their throats

until they notice their nakedness
and sign a treaty to ship them to another planet.

Out of shame

they can help plow the snow
in exchange for more juice.

To know that your goodwill
would be cheered for centuries,

for as long as the aliens do not
learn your language.

To know you would sing to the aliens
when they are bored,

it is only right that you would let ________
or ________ lead the praise songs.

But remember, there is an ember
of a broken fig in your chest.

When they refuse your proposal,
it smolders in the dark chamber.

Unload them to an alternate planet—
no one would ask when they go missing.

To know the aliens deserve Pluto,
or anywhere in space, not far from a black hole.

If they survive, that is a miracle enough.

To know you can blame them
for not dancing to your praises.

To know some of them would jump off the ship,
and they would continue to float,

that is not your fault either.
On Mars, even the living float.

The spaceship would lift
and not catch fire. This time,

if fire erupts from the emergency exit,
you may have to close your eyes in prayers,

because you already know
that Mars has no track for race.

HOMELESS

Because I woke up to a frozen neighborhood,

I wondered how   it ever bloomed
after it got so white   and lonely.

Where do the birds hide   when it snows?

I have many questions, but I only ask   my reflection
from the mirror, any time I wash my face   for another prayer.

Where do the homeless sleep when it's all cold?

In the days that followed March,
                    I pondered the miracle   of the virgin sky.

I prayed that God forever commands His doors open,
even when it didn't snow, even when the grasses rebelled.

KHALWA IN A MUSEUM

1.

In this picture,
I stood on the bank of a lake

just before I tossed a coin into it.

I imagined the eel that would swallow
the coin would get swallowed by a fish.

2.

I held a rosary in one hand
and a lantern in the other

as I walked into the circle of boys,
with whom

I learned to speak to ghosts
of the wanderers.

I stood on the bank of a lake,
dressed for a funeral, many miles from home.

3.

I sat in front of the box where Baba saved books and diaries.
I found a postcard in one of the brown envelopes.

I cried out into an empty tin, because I know
that nostalgia is the closest phase to being an angel.

I crossed the same garden many nights
until my face was greased

like a potter's supple fingers
rolling mud into a pot.

Now I know where to seek light when it's cold.

4.

Baba sat with strangers
and they wore matching clothes.

A giant tesbihi around his neck.

We bury our dead in the same cloth we pray in in
God's house.
Baba had ihram in his cupboard, and

as if to prepare us for death,

he gifted me one of those he saved for himself,
but I slept in it during harmattan.

5.

As a child, I loved this season
because
I built a cage for grasshoppers with my mother's slippers.

Every morning, I said prayers for them

and with each passing day
I buried the grasshoppers,
until there were none left.

I made a cemetery out of a garden.

Anytime I water the mimosa,
I mutter "wa inna in sha Allah, bikum lahikun."

6.

I slept on a bed
by the corridor of a labor room.

That night, all the beds were taken.

Out of the theater—
held on both sides by nurses,

a woman begged that the child be sewn back in her stomach.

It's been days.
She refused to breastfeed the baby.

Miles away from this hospital,
an exorcist waited outside his house,

chains in one hand,
Qur'an in the other.

7.

The exorcist
camouflaged in the night

and forced kubejaro down the throats
of whisperers amongst the girls and the
widows—

he blamed the sun
for the death of his hibiscus.

This is not about the garden;
he doesn't want to be inherited

to keep secret all he buried
in his yard while they slept.

The women were blamed for the death   of the
        dictator's sister
so he led an army against   what should have been his.

In this picture, I stood on the bank of a lake,
dressed for a funeral, many miles from home.

NOMAD

1.

The pigeons perched on our roof are mine / they returned / every morning as I swept the yard after the night's feast / We all belong where we want to return / or where the swooshing / of the brooms did not trigger our wings / Baba had a rusty sword / at the edge of his bed / when he unsheathed it / there had been burning car tires on our street / and muezzins are warned not to announce the arrival of dawn / Whoever God wants to make homeless / he first makes nomad / Baba paced the yard / his eyes were the size of a new moon peeking at dusk / If I own a camel / I won't travel / outside the borders of this desert / But when I think of the wind and how hard they came / against the sand / I knew thirst would lead us out some day / It was why we continued to live / in a city that swallowed seeds without making flowers/ I harbored nostalgia for those nights /

2.

Baba made ablution but permitted us / to sleep on the spread mat / Cooed by silence / we opened our eyes / to the soft knocks on our door / prayers were said in whispers / Whoever God wants to make mad / he makes shepherd / A nomad must have a tree / trusted to keep his mares safe from the storm / As they wandered with their eyes closed / among birds that chirped songs that were new to their ears / They journeyed through silky darkness / swamped with bees / and blind in the smoke / drifting / as a butterfly / unsure which will bring the most pleasure / swaying / or landing on a leaf that has sweet scent / In the wind is a whisper that lured them to sleep / The light that vanished from their eyes / would someday emerge in a well /

3.

Baba's baba left home with no map in his pocket / His bag swelled with the pages he designed / with the ink he made from sugar / and many shapes of rosaries he inherited / from dead men. Except when it was prayer time / he folded his left palm / where he held a letter that became his will / The only pages we all inherited / Baba asked me to read the commandments / to his ears / he paused at intervals to explain the lines / He saw I had made a cane / from the felled mango branch / he knew I was going to walk miles / until I cross the ghost town outside of the desert, where there's a man—trapped / within the rectangle of a mosque / he called the prayers but only men in khaki joined him / The field God lined with gold, he bordered with sleeping tombs.

CROSSROAD

1.
The river flows out of the city
through a creek where crocodiles once ruled.

Now, a congregation of boys with calabashes
designed with black tape swim in it,

in search of a fish that may never be found
until the sun sets. Here, it is taboo to

retrieve a net when the sky is pitch dark.

2.
The boy is dying of hunger.

From the photograph,
you'd think he hungers for death.

3.
He inherited a skin that is also
a cloud of smoke.

In case of emergency—which could be every day,
he'd jumped through the window, run
until his feet hit the puddle in a field.

The boy—shouted onto the sky,
as the smoke climbed and climbed
before it disappeared.

4.

The boy walked miles with wounds on his palms.
He journeyed across a desert

with a tongue inked in grief.
No one understood how

the boy survived
the committee of vultures.

A page soaked in ink is
another form of blankness.

From a lighthouse,
surrounded by bats,

the boy softened his tongue
with the prayers he learned from his mama.

5.

He learned to say goodbye
in sign language,
as he looked at his reflection in the restroom mirror—
practicing,

it flashed the picture that surfaced on Twitter —of
Egypt.

There was a knock on the door; it sounded loud
and familiar.

This reminded him of the mourners under Folawiyo
Bridge—

he witnessed as a policeman's courage widowed his lover
in Kaduna,

and the slippers   pooled at the crossroad
for weeks

outside the prayer house in Kano.

6.

Praises in haphazard rhythms
like thuds of rain   on clay.

Bones splintered and the songs from the minarets
were muffled in the raging fire.

The mirage on the footpath some days
led to the sea.

Outside the mosque, a boy searched
for his baba's missing sandals.

All the shoes are in similar sizes,
as if a man's leg could tell how his life would end.

The boy returned home;   *his palms now have enough signs for God's praises.*

7.

He mourned the ghosts that wandered the corridors of the mosque,
where they would have been after the prayers—
to fix wedding dates and debate politics
until their tongues became grungy cotton balls.

Anytime he heard the call to prayer,
he imagined ghosts gathered beneath
the lemon tree outside the mosque.

With each day,
he wondered how long the shoes will remain
before the other children   remember

to search for their father's—
the shoes will fit someday.

8.

Beneath the boy's left foot
is a sacred geometry

that could be a womb
or a graveyard.

Either is home.

His mama said the dead return home
every Thursday night.

But all he saw were
his own shadows, growing on the walls.

He sang of the days before the blast
under the bridge

but no one danced on a crumbled monument.

9.

On the clay path back home, he found a vulture—wounded, it hoped to get healed before it became preyed upon. The boy clipped its wings. That day, he prayed for a fish, but slept heavy with the peppered flesh of a bird. The ritual must be observed, a coin is placed inside the detached head of the vulture and buried with its talons. That is how you make sure none of the dead it ate would make their way into his eyes while he slept.

The boy singed the feathers, and
it burned like the flag of this country

halfway in water—
too deep to be rescued,
and too shallow to be freed from the flaming front.

He counted his fingers
and let the radio sing through the night.

All he heard   were slurps of lost frequencies.

10.
He misses the old dirty sky;
it hinted when it would rain.

No matter how hard he wailed,
the sky cannot undo its glimmer   for any death.

Begin with the boy   telling his mama that night
about the cities in his stomach   that caught fire.

Begin with the night after you heard this story.
Your exhale is an ode to the absence

of the stars   when the sky is geared for rain.

The crossroad is where the hungry met the dying,
or where a bird walked on its legs when failed by its feathers.

* *The italicized line in part 6 was inspired by the work of Raymond Antrobus.*

MIRROR

Finger marks
      on a tray
of sea sand.

At my naming ceremony, I was announced as a child with dual stripes of faith and shame for a body that mirrored a fantasy house. Ẹni ku ati ẹni sọnu ma pádé l'ọjọ kan. I wondered if the ghosts of the dead would miss their way back home, or if the missing would be assumed dead. Their meeting is the motivation for the pilgrimage. Baba swore by the curtains and the sky that he saw his dead mother in hajj.

But when I left home,
it was not in search of my dead.

I listened to Baba's prophecy about the tiger in me. I asked, how come
      it never roars?

When I'm lonely, the tiger in me eats veggies,
or drags its sharp claws on its own skin—
in me is a predator that haunts itself.

The picture in the mirror was not in the mirror—
the tiger was
a cat—furred with loneliness.

A lone star
sits on the fall sky

as I bury what I love.

I located the shovels

in the field
of hay waiting to be trimmed.

In soft steps,
I walked the path

between each grave,
until I had enough.

My brothers held a metal bucket, ran toward the pole that must be pedaled until its borehole releases enough water to make paste of the sand. There was a crowd of older men who asked us to lodge the sand until it became like the roof of a castle submerged in a sandstorm. Before we left, I dropped the shovel where I took the last heap of sand. Someone else would retrace the distance between each buried body for the bucket and the planks. They—unlike us—would peek at the sky for the specks of light. They would pray for it to rain, because they had planted maize seedlings the day before, but no one prays for rain before they bury their dead.

Prayers were said
by men who hid their wavering
in large frocks

and whispered elegies,
as if anticipating a miracle.

Outside the gate,
a man sweetened a bag of cotton,
he gave it out in exchange for pill bottles.
He squeezed the horn in his hands, like a train
announcing its departure.
He waved as our hearse drove by,
he offered me a bite, to heal my wounds.
I smiled, and he smiled back. That was enough condolence.

Thinned out,
his image in the mirror is
no longer in the mirror.

Undone by the fading of smiles on the faces of men who knew how to sweeten the mouth better than their wounds. Now I understand the curiosity of a collared dove striking its beak on my window. Once, I thought it wanted to crack its way in. Now I know I've always been wrong. It sought to unveil the feathers only the mirror could see beneath its reflection.

If I stare too long,
staring at my bathroom mirror,
I should see the stripes of a tiger,
but it will remain nameless
until the day I die,
before the elegies
are sung by men
who would go back
to the tray of sand,
seeking to know
if I want someone else
named after me.

BOUQUET

For centuries,
petals

held
encrypted

messages,
until the mouth

formed
enough
alphabets for love.

Before there was hay, there was a field.

The genesis
of everything
beautiful
is light—
or rain
or both.

Whatever hints of love, hints of death.

ACKNOWLEDGMENTS

The following poems have been published previously:

"Ashes," *Tupelo Quarterly*, March 2022, www.tupeloquarterly.com

"Autobiography Inside a Church," *Hobart*, December 12, 2017, www.hobartpulp.com

"Beach," *Poetry Magazine*, February 2024

"Birds," *African Writer Magazine*, Special Issue no. 1 (January 2021), www.AfricanWriter.com

"Birthmark," *Split Lip Magazine*, 2018

"Bouquet," "Circle," and "Reflection," *Efiko Magazine*, February 19, 2023, https://efikomag.com

"Chimera (Palm and Wine)," *Denver Quarterly* 56, no. 4 (2022)

"Departure," *Tupelo Quarterly*, March 2022, www.tupeloquarterly.com

"Gravity," *The America Poetry Review* 52, no. 3 (2023)

"Gray" (as "Empty"), *The Los Angeles Review*, April 17, 2023, https://losangelesreview.org

"Homeless," *The Common*, no. 24 (2022)

"Incantation for a Lake," *A Public Space*, no. 31 (December 2023)

"Incantation for the Drowned," *Gulf Coast Journal* 35, no. 2 (2023)

"Khalwa in a Museum" (as "Incantation II"), *Memorious* 33 (2023), https://memorious.org

"Mirror" (as "Sand Therapy"), *Southern Humanities Review*, 56, no. 3 (Fall 2023)

"Monologue in a Library" and "Palsy," *Cherry Tree: A National Literary Journal @ Washington College*, no. 4 (2018)

"Nomad," *Gordon Square Review* 12 (2023)

"North," *Ninth Letter* 19, no. 2 (2022–23)

"Radio," *Southern Humanities Review* 56, no. 1 (2023)

"Taxonomy: Grief," *Connotation Press: An Online Artifact*, 2019, www.connotationpress.com

"Unmarked," *Willow Springs* 90 (Fall 2022)

"Yoruba Abecedarian" (as "Yoruba Abecedarian I"), *Poetry Wales*, December 14, 2022, https://poetrywales.co.uk

My thanks to Ruth Awad for selecting "Nomad" as the winner of the 2023 *Gordon Square Review* poetry contest, to Joy Harjo for selecting "Mirror" (as "Sand Therapy") as runner-up for the 2023 Auburn Witness Poetry Prize at *Southern Humanities Review*, and to the University of Mississippi Department of English for recognizing my work with the 2023 Bondurant Prize for poetry by an MFA student.

Sincere appreciation to the entire Department of English at the University of Cincinnati as well as the following faculty for their suggestions and support throughout the course of writing this book: Rebecca Lindenberg, Aditi Machado, Simone Nicole Savannah, and Felicia Zamora.

Thanks to Sean Cho Ayres, Blessing Christopher, Asher Marron, Hassan Mirza, Rome Hernandez Morgan, Dior Stephens, and Andy Sia.

As always, thanks to my family, to my wife, Zainab Omolola Bello, and to Mutmainnah Oluwakemi.

My sincere gratitude to Marisa Emily Siegel, who first saw the light in this book, and to Robin Hoffman, whose keen eyes fine-tuned it. Thank you to Charlotte Keathley, Madeline Schultz, Maia Rigas, Courtney Smotherman, and the whole team at Northwestern University Press for their unwavering support and commitment to the publication of this book.